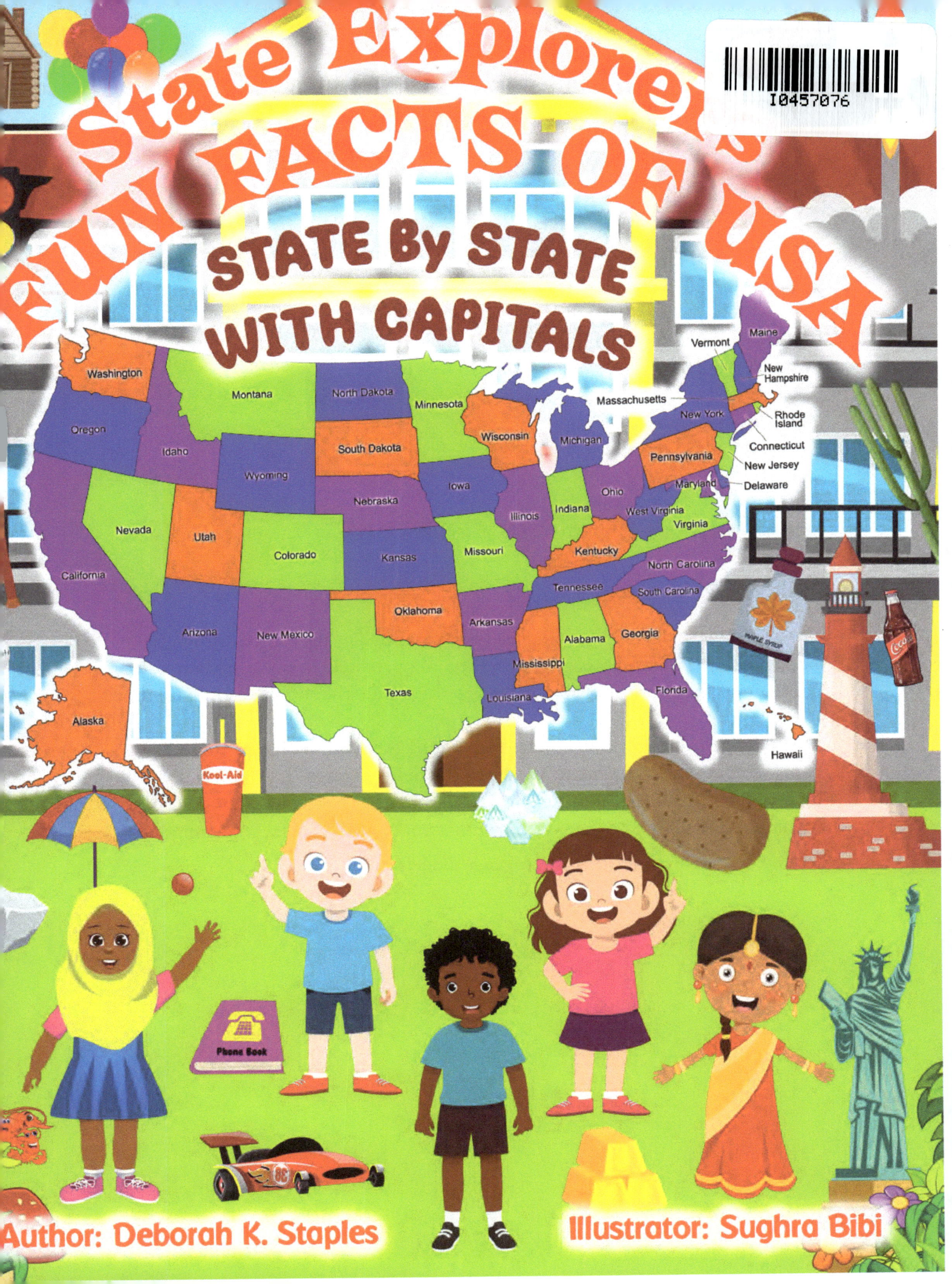

State Explorers: Fun Facts of USA State By State With Capitals
Copyright © 2025, by Deborah K. Staples

ISBN: 979-8-218-63111-6 (Hardback)
ISBN: 979-8-218-90995-6 (Paperback)

Published by: Joy Walker Ministry
Printed in the United States of America

Illustrations By: Sughra Bibi
Facts about the states were retrieved from Reader's Digest and Infoplease

All rights reserved.

No part of this book may be reproduced or transmitted in any form electronic, or mechanical, including photocopying and recording, or held in any information storage and retrieval system without permission in writing from the author and publisher.

NO AI TRAINING: Without in any way limiting the author's [and publisher's] exclusive rights under copyright, any use of this publication to "train" generative artificial intelligence (AI) technologies to generate text is expressly prohibited. The author reserves all rights to license uses of this work for generative AI training and development of machine learning language models.

WHAT EDUCATORS AND PARENTS ARE SAYING

This book is thoughtfully designed for children, making it an excellent resource for early readers and learners. It also provides informative historical facts that enhance understanding.

Cheryl M. Jones, Principal and
Tayana A. Patterson, Interventionisty/Instructional Coach

This educational book takes young scholars on a journey across the United States providing fun facts enjoyable for all ages. The book has diverse characters which is impoprtant, as children need to see themselves portrayed in their learning.

As an eduator, this book is a wonderful resource to introduce students to geography and could allow them to perform their own research at a developmentally appropriate level.

Brooke Mills, Elementary Teacher

ACKNOWLEDGEMENTS

To Sughra Bibi, my illustrator, thank you very much.

Special thanks to my spiritual brother Julius T. Myricks, who encouraged me to teach, believe in, and bring creativity to children across the world. Your advice, knowledge and wisdom will follow children as they turn the pages in this book and learn so many fun facts about the world they live in.

Special thanks to Readers Digest and Infoplease for their resources on American History.

Thanks to anyone whom I may have missed, there are so many people who have contributed to my success.

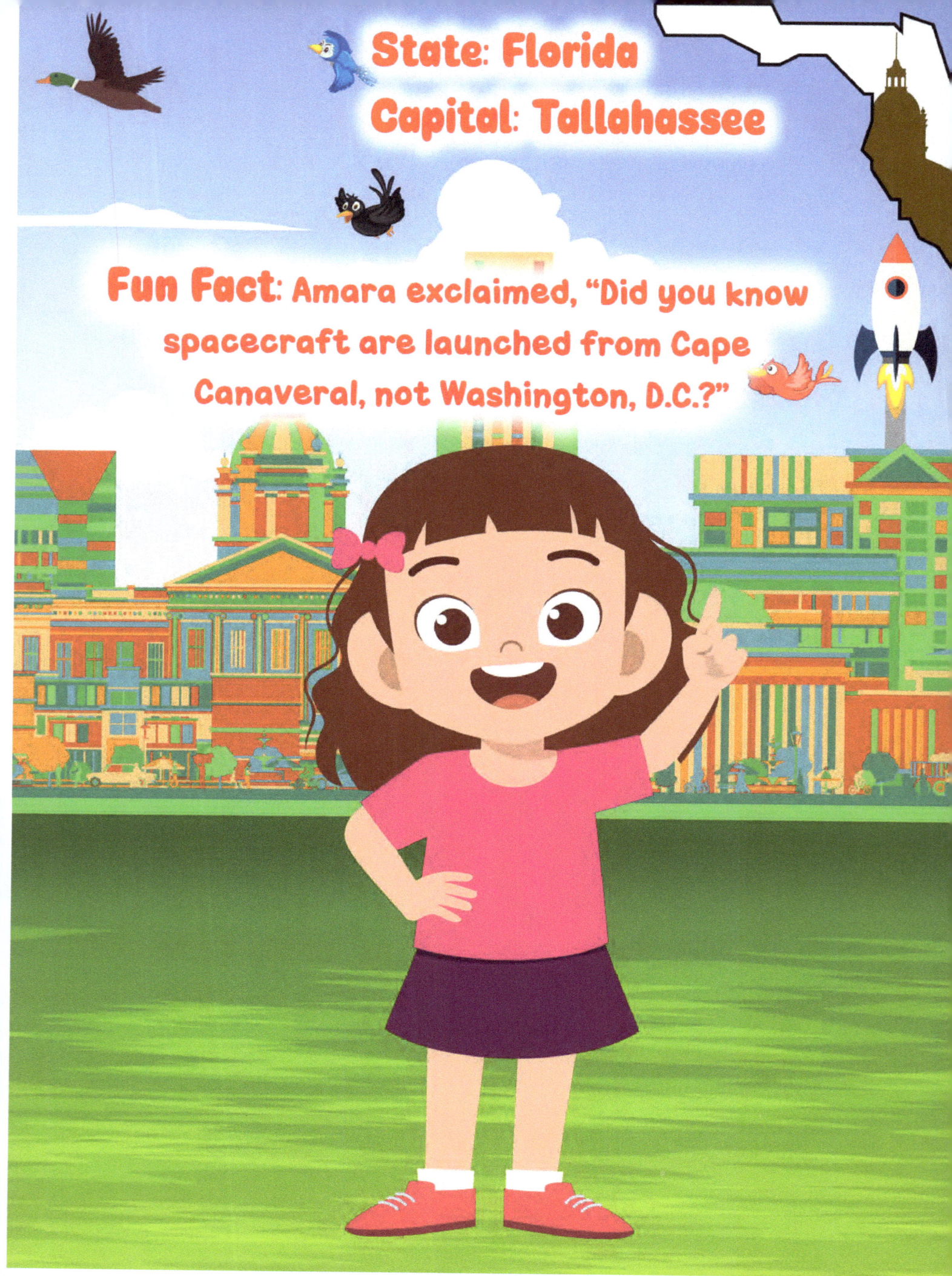

State: Iowa

Capital: Des Moines

Fun Fact: Fatima asks, "Did you know Iowa has the shortest and steepest railroad in Dubuque?"

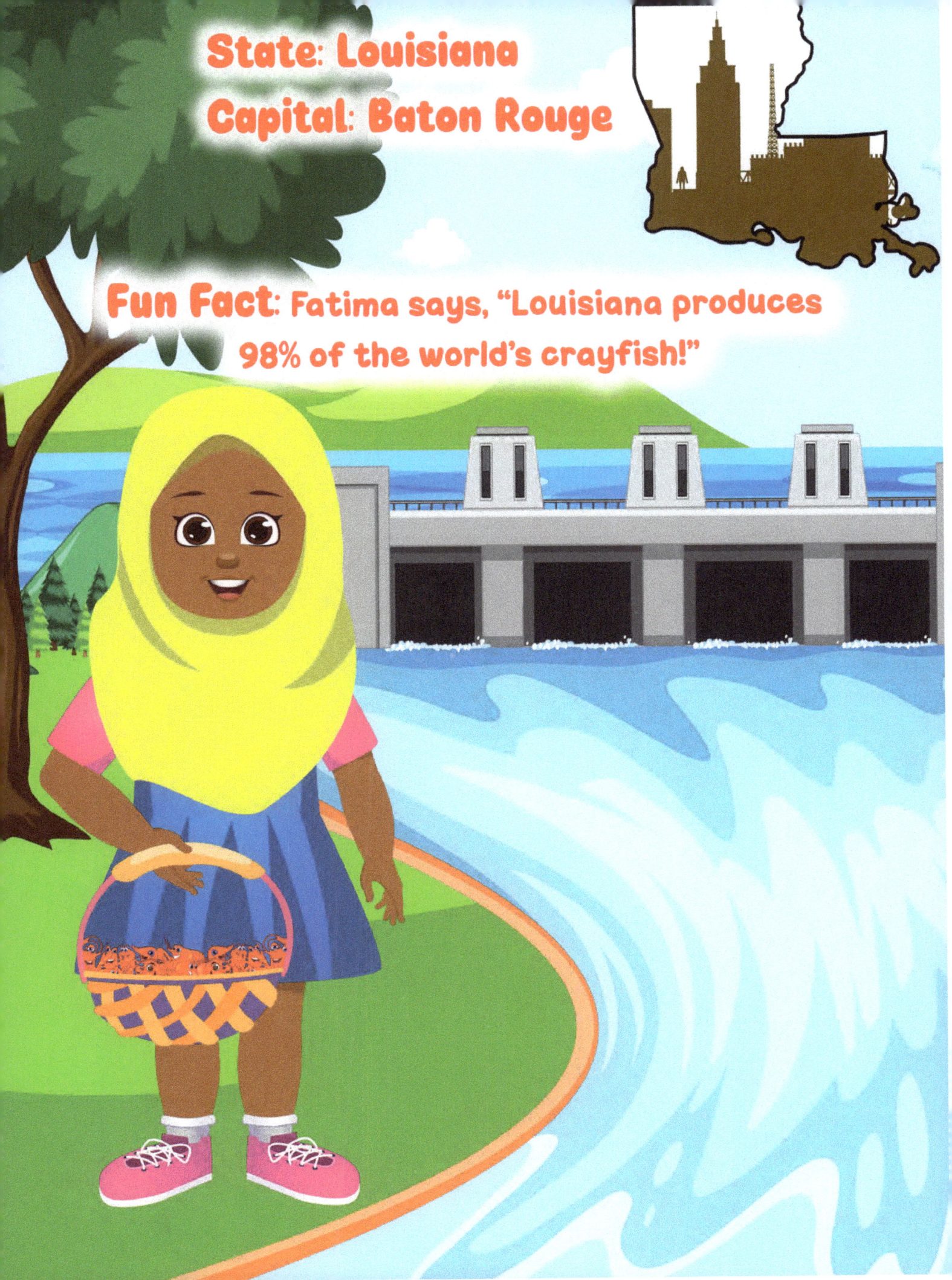

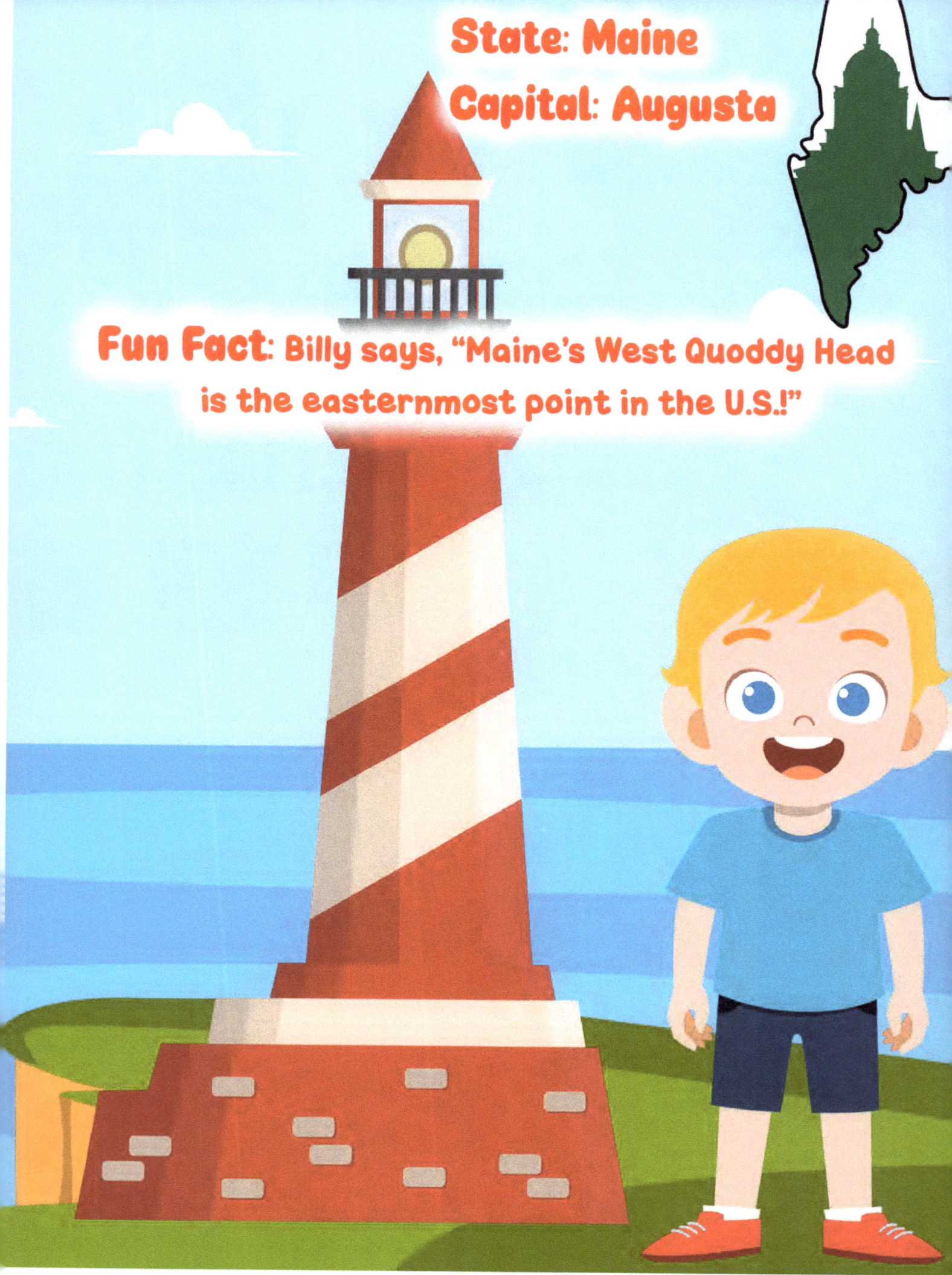

State: Massachusetts
Capital: Boston

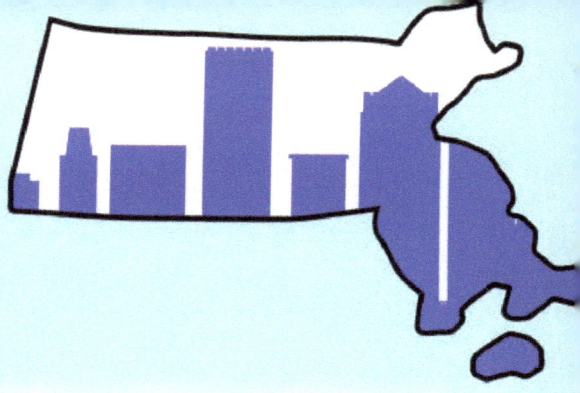

Fun Fact: Amara shouts, "The first World Series was held in Boston in 1903!"

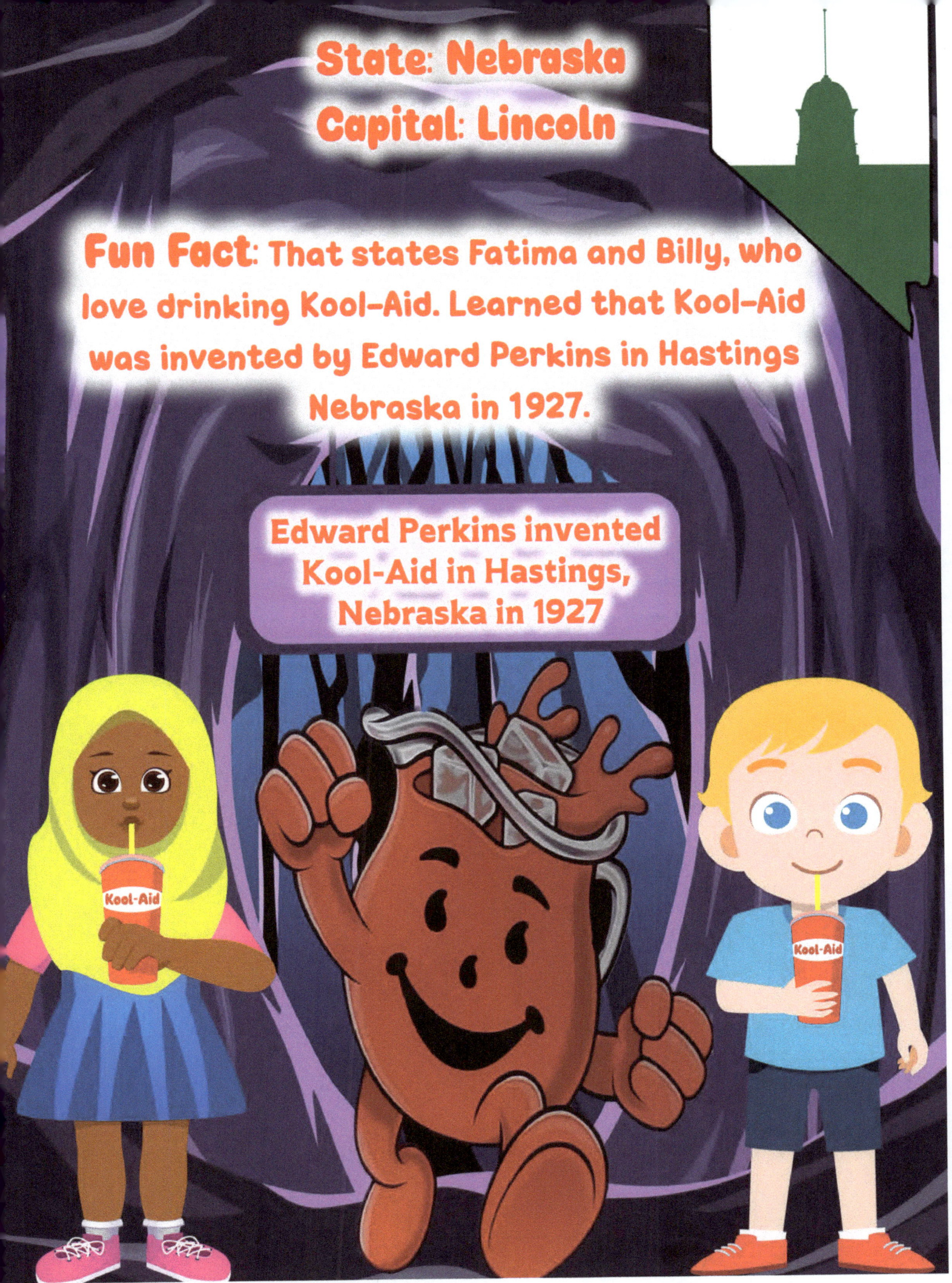

State: North Dakota
Capital: Bismarck

Fun Fact: They learned that in 2007, North Dakota set the Guinness World Record for 8,962 people making snow angels at the same time

State: Pennsylvania
Capital: Harrisburg

Fun Fact: Fatima and Amara learned that the first magazine in America was published in Philadelphia!

State: Texas
Capital: Austin

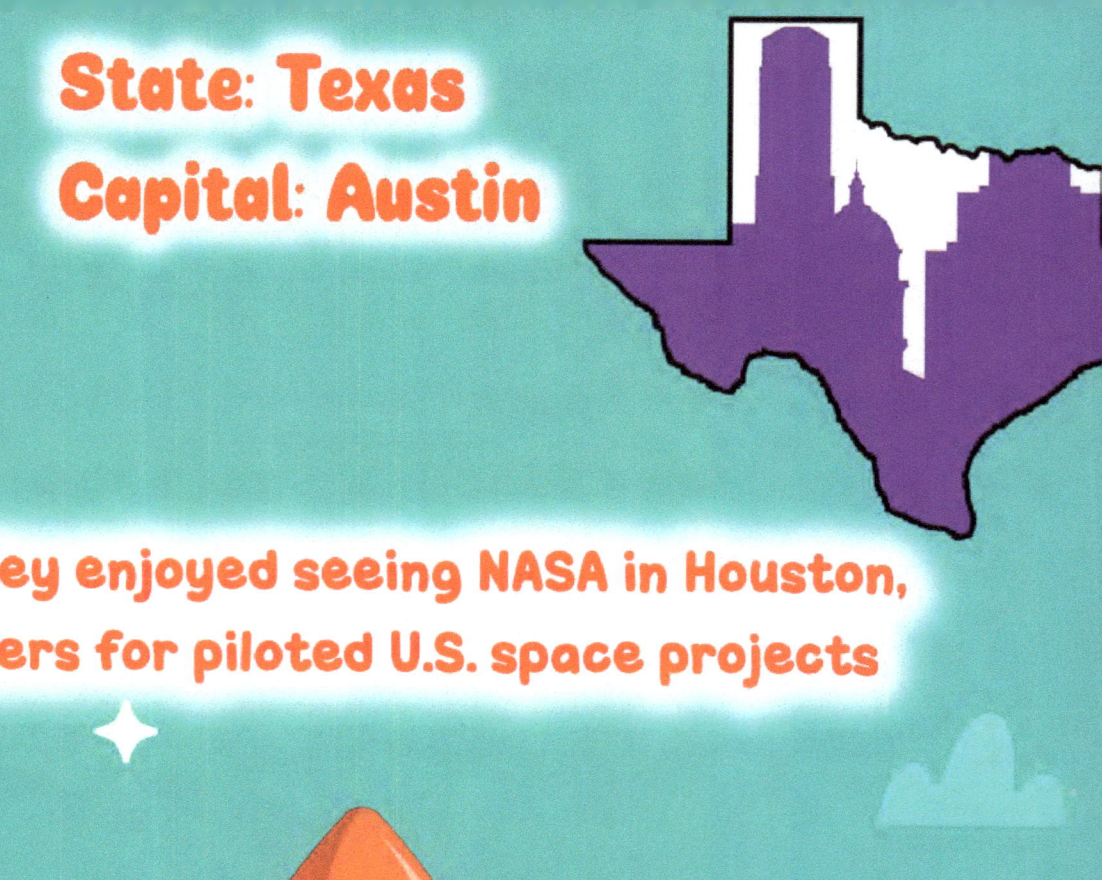

Fun Fact: They enjoyed seeing NASA in Houston, headquarters for piloted U.S. space projects

State: **Utah**
Capital: **Salt Lake City**

Fun Fact: Billy told them about the Cleveland-Lloyd Dinosaur Quarry, which holds over 12,000 dinosaur bones!

State: Washington
Capital: Olympia

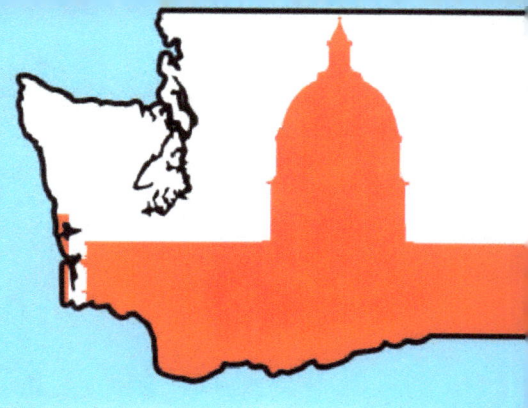

Fun Fact: Billy and Chris discovered that Boeing in Seattle makes aircraft and spacecraft!

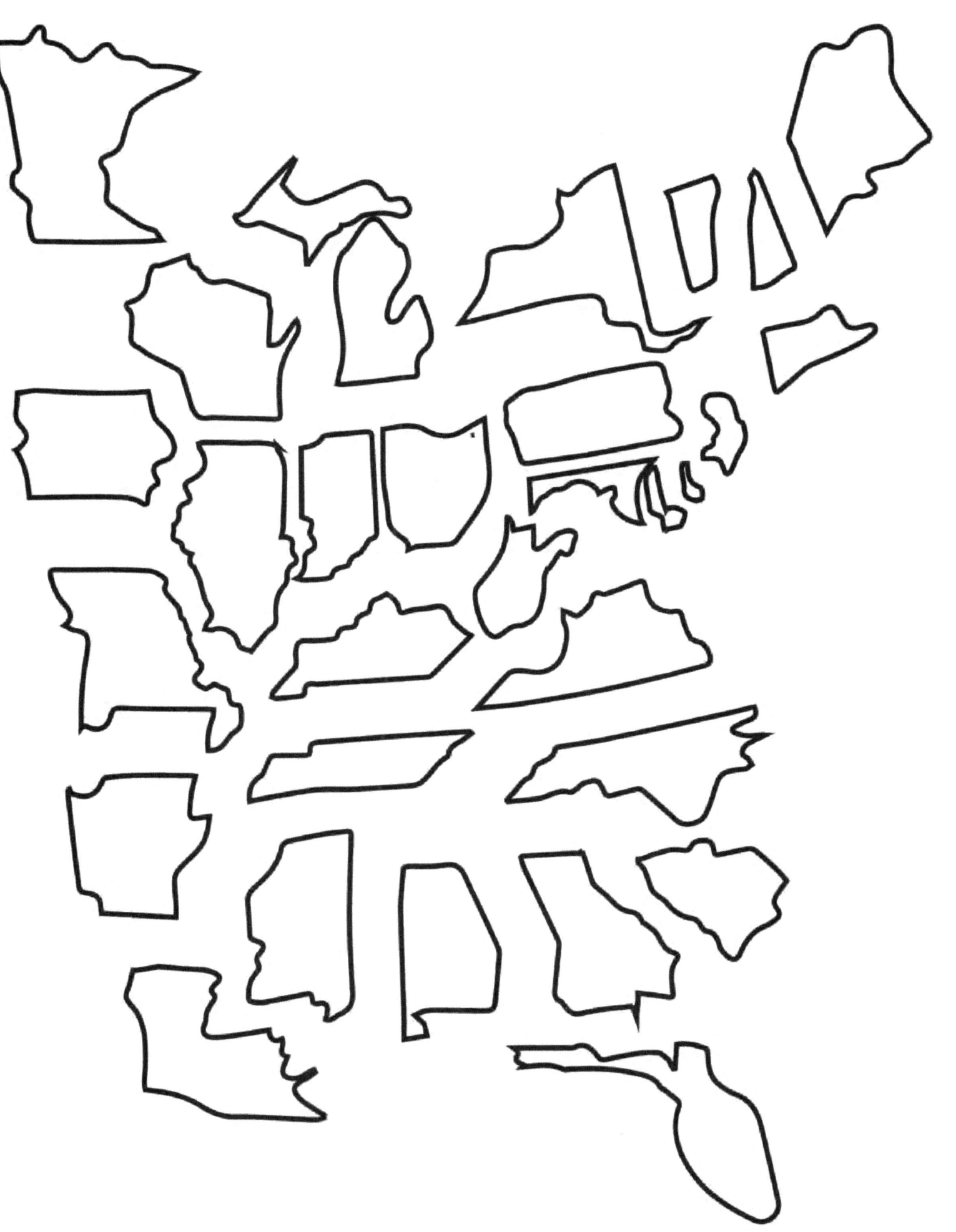

Deborah K. Staples, M.Ed., has 26 years of teaching experience. She has served as a Kindergarten teacher and a professional development trainer. Helping children learn is a passion for Deborah because she believes that learning is important. Her desire as an educator is to expose children to information that will encourage their creativity, inspire them to explore, and open their minds to a higher level of thinking.

In this edition of State Explorers, Deborah uses Fatima, Billy, Chris, Amara, and Priya to teach young children fun facts about the states around the world.

In her spare time, Ms. Staples enjoys spending time volunteering in classrooms.

www.ingramcontent.com/pod-product-compliance
Lightning Source LLC
Chambersburg PA
CBHW041521120626
46551CB00018B/2526